This book belongs to

_____

**This book is dedicated to my children – Mikey, Kobe, and Jojo.
Regardless of our differences, we are all part of the human race.**

Diversity Ninja

By Mary Nhin

Pictures by
Jelena Stupar

"Why was 6 afraid of 7?" asked Inclusive Ninja.

"I dont know," replied Diversity NInja.

"Because 7, 8, 9," said Inclusive Ninja and they both laughed hysterically.

The two friends were telling jokes during lunch.
Diversity and Inclusive Ninja have been friends since they were babies.

They have the same teachers and play the same sports.

They love the same games and watch the same tv shows.

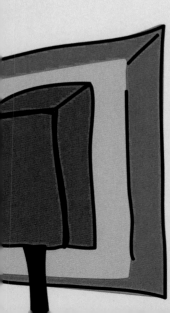

Even their favorite color is the same.

But there is one difference.

Diversity Ninja's skin color is brown and Inclusive Ninja's skin color is peach.

After lunch, the ninjas go outside to play.

The other ninjas are choosing teams for a game except Diversity Ninja doesn't get picked.

Because of his skin color, some ninjas aren't nice to Diversity Ninja. The ninjas doing it may not even realize it hurts him.

Some ninjas think just because his skin color is different, it means Diversity Ninja is not as good as them.

That's called racism.

Racism is the belief that a particular race or skin color is better than another.

When it happens, it makes Diversity Ninja feel sad.

In class, Mrs. Smith asks everyone to break up in groups of twos or threes for a class project.

The ninjas find their partners and pair up.

"Oh, Inclusive Ninja's going to be my partner," says Hangry Ninja.

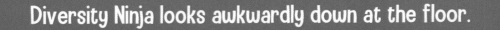

Diversity Ninja looks awkwardly down at the floor.

"So cool!" says Hangry Ninja. "What kind of story should we write?"

Inclusive Ninja and Diversity Ninja look at each other and smile.

They're both thinking the same thing.

When they get done, they present it to their class.

We may be different, but deep down we're all the same.

We all have different mouths. Some of us may use our mouths to talk while some may not talk at all. But we are all the same because we use our mouths to eat and smile.

We all talk differently. Some of us speak a different language and some of use our hands to speak. But we're the same because we all communicate our thoughts and feelings through some kind of language.

We all have different body shapes and sizes. Some of us are tall, short, wide, or narrow.

Some of us are limited in our movement.

But we are all the same because our bodies house our hearts and organs so we can live and enjoy life.

Our skin is different colors. But our skin is the same because we all use it to feel things. With our skin we can tell if something is hot, cold, wet, or dry.

Our skin performs an important function by protecting us from bacteria. Our skin regulates our body temperature by sweating when we're hot and giving us 'goosebumps' when we're cold.

Our feelings and emotions may be different at any given time.

See, look at Angry Ninja. He's angry.

And Grumpy Ninja, he's grumpy.

Don't forget Positive Ninja.
She's always positive.

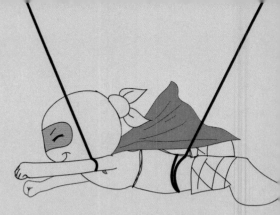

But we're the same because we all experience the same emotions – anger, positivity, grumpiness, stress, anxiety, gratitude, and confidence.

Our differences are like the colors in a rainbow and that's what makes rainbows so pretty. Being different and having diversity is a beautiful thing.

We may be different in our abilities, background, gender, or skin color, but we are all part of the human race.

Your best weapon against racism and prejudice is to practice diversity and inclusion.

Diversity promotes creativity, perspective, wisdom, and ideas.

Check out the Ninja Life Hacks Journal on Amazon to practice your diversity and inclusion skills!

 @marynhin @GrowGrit
#NinjaLifeHacks

 Mary Nhin Grow Grit

 Grow Grit

Made in the USA
Columbia, SC
15 October 2020

22917561R00020